The Larry Lea
Could You Not Tarry One Hour?
Prayer Diary

The Larry Lea Could You Not Tarry One Hour? Prayer Diary

To accompany
Could You Not Tarry One Hour?
by Larry Lea
with Judy Doyle, Ed.D.

Creation House
Strang Communications Company
Altamonte Springs, FL 32714

Copyright © 1987 by Larry Lea
All rights reserved.
Printed in the United States of America
Library of Congress Catalog Card Number: 87-071209
International Standard Book Number: 0-88419-199-0

Creation House
Strang Communications Company
190 N. Westmonte Drive
Altamonte Springs, FL 32714
(305) 869-5005

This book or parts thereof may not be reproduced in any form without permission of the publisher.

Unless otherwise noted all scriptures are from the King James Version of the Bible.

Presented to:

Name _____

Address _____

City _____

State _____

Zip _____

Phone _____

A Message From Larry Lea........................9

Using Your Prayer Diary........................11

Prayer Guide: Could You Not Tarry One Hour?..........15

Scriptures for Building Faith.....................17

How to Develop an Effective Prayer Life...............25

How to Read the Bible Through in One Year...........181

How to Pray for Missionaries and Other Christian Leaders..183

Biography..................................191

A Message From Larry Lea

"Could you not tarry one hour?" This is the question our Lord asked His disciples. It is also the question He posed to me in 1972. When I asked the Lord, "How can I pray an hour?" I remembered that Jesus instructed His disciples, "After this manner therefore pray ye" (Matt. 6:9). What we have traditionally called the Lord's Prayer has become for me a model prayer.

As I obeyed the call to pray, the Holy Spirit revealed secrets of prayer. I learned how to worship the Lord and to make powerful faith declarations based upon His names and promises. I discovered how to pray in God's provision and how to get along with everybody all the time. I learned how to pray a hedge of protection about myself, my family and my possessions, and how to stand in the victory Jesus has won for me. I put these prayer secrets into seven tapes and a 112-page study guide entitled *Could You Not Tarry One Hour?* The material is influencing the prayer lives of thousands.

Remember the passage in Ephesians 6 where Paul instructs us to put on the whole armor of God? Part of that armor is the sword of the Spirit, which is the word (*rhema*) of God (see Eph. 6:17). In this verse the reference is not to the entire Bible as such, but to the individual revelation which the Spirit brings to our minds at that particular time of need. That *rhema* word—God's specific statement, command or instruction for that particular situation—is the sword with which we can drive back and destroy the enemy!

God's words also reveal His will. We must know God's will in order to pray effectively: "And this is the confidence that we have in him, that, if we ask any thing according to his will, he heareth us: and if we know that he hear us, whatsoever we ask, we know that we have the petitions that we desired of him" (1 John 5:14,15).

Therefore, we must find God's will, come into agreement with that will and speak it in prayer if we are to pray effectively.

In times past God spoke from the outside in; now He speaks from the inside out. God wants to speak to you, but you need the vehicle of prayer, for God does not reveal Himself to casual inquirers. As you develop a praying spirit, God will begin to speak to you, for Jesus declared, "My sheep hear my voice" (John 10:27). Just as sheep abide near their shepherd day after day and learn to recognize and obey his voice, so we must learn to dwell near our Shepherd if we are to become intimately acquainted with His voice and His ways.

Are you tired of getting your second orders? Of being out of the will of God? Ask God to give you ears that can hear His voice; then when He speaks, write down His creative words to you. As you learn to hear His voice and obey it, the Holy Spirit will lead you into paths of freedom, joy and peace.

"Faith cometh by hearing, and hearing by the word of God" (Rom. 10:17). This means that information has a whole lot to do with inspiration. Take your next step. Seek God daily in prayer, and pray that you will have hearing ears. Why? Because once you hear His voice, all you have to do is obey!

That is why I have included a place in this prayer diary for you to record what the Lord speaks to your heart as you pray. When the Spirit of God flashes a revelation, scripture or command into your spirit, take a moment to write it down and then continue praying. Treasure God's words to you. Declare them aloud. Use them as a sharp sword to drive back the enemy and defeat him!

Don't forget to keep a record of the specific timing of your prayer requests, as well as God's answers. This record will enable you to look back and see God's faithfulness in answering prayer. It will also help you understand and trust His wisdom in withholding or delaying some answers. Reviewing past answers to prayer will build your faith, remind you not to take God's blessings for granted and fill your mouth with praise and thanksgiving as you bring new requests to Him (see Phil. 4:6).

May God bless you as you use this prayer diary to enrich your prayer life and to develop hearing ears!

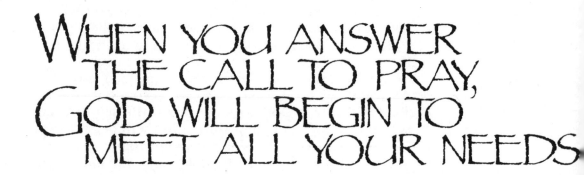

WHEN YOU ANSWER THE CALL TO PRAY, GOD WILL BEGIN TO MEET ALL YOUR NEEDS

Using Your Prayer Diary

Two stubborn problems confront the Christian struggling to learn the joy of prayer: knowing *how* to pray and developing the *discipline* to pray. This prayer diary attacks both problems.

Interruptions, fatigue and pressures often drown out the call to pray. But discipline can be developed by training yourself to translate problems and pressures into specific, written requests and by recording every answer to prayer. The pages of your prayer diary are undated so you can tailor it to your own personal needs as you learn not to worry about anything, but to pray about everything.

However, it is hard to develop the *discipline* to pray if you do not know *how* to pray. That is probably the root of your broken vows and frustrating efforts in the past. Therefore, if you want to enter into the joy of prayer, you must learn how and what to pray.

If you've glanced through this prayer diary, you have discovered it is based on the Lord's Prayer. What we have traditionally called the Lord's Prayer is actually a model prayer in which Jesus outlines six topics as a pattern to be followed under the guidance of the Holy Spirit. These six topics should be included in our daily prayer time, for they cover all our needs.

The prayer outline based on the Lord's Prayer is included on pages 15-16 in this prayer diary. Larry Lea recommends using it as a pattern. If you have not used the outline before, the following brief explanation will help you learn how to pray according to the model prayer Jesus gave us.

Promises — Our Father which art in heaven, Hallowed be thy name.

The Lord's Prayer opens with praise; therefore, at this first topic, praise the Lord and appropriate His promises. Thank God for sending His Son to redeem you, for if it weren't for Jesus, you could not call God Father (Gal. 4:4-6).

Then hallow the name of God by agreeing with who our Father is and what He has already done in Jesus Christ. At this point, you may want to include eight Hebrew names for God in your praises. (See prayer outline.) These names correspond with the fivefold promise God makes to His people under the new covenant which is fulfilled in the person and work of Christ. Through praise, you enter into the very presence of God, opening the way to bring your petitions before Him.

Priorities
Thy kingdom come.
Thy will be done.

God reigns over you when you obey Him and accept His will and authority in your life. Therefore, at this second topic, declare that God's kingdom (His righteousness, joy and peace—Rom. 14:17) shall come and that His will and priorities shall be established in these four areas: (1) yourself, (2) your loved ones, (3) your church and (4) your nation. Pray over each of these areas, one by one.

Provision
Give us this day our daily bread.

There are four basic requirements for appropriating God's provision for your physical and material needs. You must *be in the will of God* and seek first the kingdom of God and His righteousness. You must claim God's promises and *believe it is God's will to prosper you*, for this will give you confidence to come daily before the Lord with your needs. Third, you must *be specific*. Don't pray in generalities. Make definite requests. Fourth, *be tenacious*. Keep praying until your answer comes. Refuse to let discouragement or unbelief rob you of your answers to prayer.

People
Forgive us our debts as we forgive our debtors.

Ask God to forgive your wrong relationships, attitudes, etc. You must forgive and release others if you want God to forgive you and remove your sin, guilt and tormenting memories. In prayer each day, set your will to forgive anyone who wrongs you.

Power
And lead us not into temptation, but deliver us from evil.

At the beginning of every day, you should pray a hedge of protection about yourself, your loved ones and your possessions. In Psalm 91 are three reasons—or "becauses"—why you can claim God's protection: (1) "Because thou hast made the Lord...thy habitation"—v. 9; (2) "Because he hath set his love upon me"—v. 14; and (3) "Because he hath known my name"—v. 14. Make certain each day that you are walking in these three bases for God's protection.

You should also put on the whole armor of God, as outlined in Ephesians 6:14-17, by believing and declaring who Jesus, your armor of light, is (Rom. 13:12,14). (See prayer outline.) Fully clad in the armor of God and encircled by God's hedge of protection, you can stand secure in the victory Jesus has won for you.

Praise | For thine is the kingdom, and the power, and the glory for ever. Amen.

When we come to this last prayer topic, we should praise God because He has invited us to be participants in His kingdom (2 Tim. 4:18; Luke 12:32), His power (Ps. 68:35; Luke 10:19), and His glory (2 Cor. 3:18; Heb. 2:9-10). We should never enter or leave God's presence without humbly bowing before Him and offering a sacrifice of praise.

Pray as Jesus taught us to pray. Use this prayer diary to record your prayer requests, your answers to prayer and the *rhema* words given to you by the Holy Spirit. You will be amazed at the dramatic increases in the effectiveness of your prayer ministry and the deepening of your relationship with the Lord.

Prayer Guide: Could You Not Tarry One Hour?

I. Promises
Our Father which art in heaven, Hallowed be thy name.

A. Picture Calvary and thank God you can call Him Father by virtue of the blood of Jesus.
B. Hallow the names of God corresponding with the five benefits in the new covenant, and make your faith declarations.

Benefit	Name	Meaning
Sin	*Jehovah-tsidkenu*	The Lord My Righteousness
	Jehovah-m'kaddesh	The Lord Who Sanctifies
Spirit	*Jehovah-shalom*	The Lord Is Peace
	Jehovah-shammah	The Lord Is There
Soundness	*Jehovah-rophe*	The Lord Who Heals
Success	*Jehovah-jireh*	The Lord's Provision Shall Be Seen
Security	*Jehovah-nissi*	The Lord My Banner
	Jehovah-rohi	The Lord My Shepherd

II. Priorities
Thy kingdom come. Thy will be done.

A. Yourself
B. Your family (mate, children, other family members)
C. Your church (pastor, leadership, faithfulness of the people, harvest)
D. Nation (city, state and national political and spiritual leaders, a specific nation)

III. Provision
Give us this day our daily bread.

A. Be in the will of God (prayer life, church, work habits, obedience in giving).
B. Believe it is God's will to prosper you.
C. Be specific.
D. Be tenacious.

IV. People — *And forgive us our debts as we forgive our debtors.*

   A. Ask God to forgive you.
   B. Forgive and release others.
   C. Set your will to forgive those who sin against you.

V. Power — *And lead us not into temptation, but deliver us from evil.*

   A. Put on the whole armor of God, the Lord Jesus Christ.
     1. Loins girt about with truth
     2. Breastplate of righteousness
     3. Feet shod with the preparation (readiness) of the gospel of peace
     4. Shield of faith
     5. Helmet of salvation
     6. Sword of the Spirit which is the Word (*rhema*) of God
   B. Pray a hedge of protection. (The Lord is your refuge, your fortress, your God; in Him will you trust.)
     1. Because you have made the Lord your habitation
     2. Because you have set your love upon Him
     3. Because you have known His name

VI. Praise — *For thine is the kingdom, and the power, and the glory, for ever.*

   A. Make your faith declarations.
   B. Return to praise.

Scriptures for Building Faith

ur heavenly Father has provided a marvelous inheritance for His children. **He has given us all things that pertain unto life and godliness: physical, spiritual,** material and personal blessings (2 Pet. 1:3,4). The Bible, God's will and testament, contains hundreds of precious promises to which believers are heirs. But like any inheritance, God's blessings and gifts must be claimed if they are to be of any benefit. We receive our inheritance by reading and meditating upon God's promises, claiming them as our own by turning them into prayers and faith declarations and receiving them by faith.

The following scriptures are provided to help you become accustomed to appropriating God's promises as you pray.

1. Promises

"Our Father which art in heaven, Hallowed be Thy name."

***Jehovah-tsidkenu*, "The Lord Our Righteousness"**

"For he hath made him to be sin for us, who knew no sin; that we might be made the righteousness of God in him" (2 Cor. 5:21).

"For Christ also hath once suffered for sins, the just for the unjust, that he might bring us to God, being put to death in the flesh, but quickened by the Spirit" (1 Pet. 3:18).

"For if by one man's offence death reigned by one; much more they which receive abundance of grace and of the gift of righteousness shall reign in life by one, Jesus Christ. Therefore as by the offence of one judgment came upon all men to condemnation; even so by the righteousness of one the free gift came upon all men unto justification of life. For as by one man's disobedience many were made sinners, so by the obedience of one shall many be made righteous" (Rom. 5:17-19).

***Jehovah-m'kaddesh*, "The Lord Who Sanctifies"**

"But of him are ye in Christ Jesus, who of God is made unto us wisdom, and righteousness, and sanctification, and redemption" (1 Cor. 1:30).

"But if we walk in the light, as he is in the light, we have fellowship one with another, and the blood of Jesus Christ his Son cleanseth us from all sin....If we confess our sins, he is faithful and just to forgive us our sins, and to cleanse us from all unrighteousness" (1 John 1:7,9).

"Know ye not that the unrighteous shall not inherit the kingdom of God? Be not deceived: neither fornicators, nor idolaters, nor adulterers, nor effeminate, nor abusers of themselves with mankind, nor thieves, nor covetous, nor drunkards, nor revilers, nor extortioners, shall inherit the kingdom of God. And such were some of you: but ye are washed, but ye are sanctified, but ye are justified in the name of the Lord Jesus, and by the Spirit of our God" (1 Cor. 6:9-11).

"And the very God of peace sanctify you wholly; and I pray God your whole spirit and soul and body be preserved blameless unto the coming of our Lord Jesus Christ" (1 Thess. 5:23).

"Wherefore Jesus also, that he might sanctify the people with his own blood, suffered without the gate" (Heb. 13:12).

Jehovah-shalom, "The Lord Is Peace"

"And, having made peace through the blood of his cross, by him to reconcile all things unto himself; by him, I say, whether they be things in earth, or things in heaven. And you, that were sometime alienated and enemies in your mind by wicked works, yet now hath he reconciled in the body of his flesh through death, to present you holy and unblameable and unreproveable in his sight" (Col. 1:20-22).

"Be careful for nothing; but in everything by prayer and supplication with thanksgiving let your requests be made known unto God. And the peace of God, which passeth all understanding, shall keep your hearts and minds through Christ Jesus" (Phil. 4:6,7).

"For God hath not given us the spirit of fear; but of power, and of love, and of a sound mind" (2 Tim. 1:7).

Jehovah-shammah, "The Lord Is There"

"Know ye not that ye are the temple of God, and the Spirit of God dwelleth in you?" (1 Cor. 3:16).

"...For he hath said, I will never leave thee, nor forsake thee. So that we may boldly say, The Lord is my helper, and I will not fear what man shall do unto me" (Heb. 13:5,6).

Jehovah-rophe, "The Lord Who Heals"

"But he was wounded for our transgressions, he was bruised for our iniquities: the chastisement of our peace was upon him; and with his stripes we are healed" (Is. 53:5).

"Who his own self bare our sins in his own body on the tree, that we, being dead to sins, should live unto righteousness: by whose stripes ye were healed" (1 Pet. 2:24).

"And ye shall serve the Lord your God, and he shall bless thy bread, and thy water; and I will take sickness away from the midst of thee. There shall nothing cast their young, nor be barren, in thy land: the number of thy days I will fulfill" (Ex. 23:25,26).

Jehovah-jireh, "The Lord's Provision Shall Be Seen"

"For the law of the Spirit of life in Christ Jesus hath made me free from the law of sin and death" (Rom. 8:2).

"Christ hath redeemed us from the curse of the law, being made a curse for us: for it is written, Cursed is every one that hangeth on a tree: that the blessing of Abraham might come on the Gentiles through Jesus Christ; that we might receive the promise of the Spirit through faith" (Gal. 3:13,14).

"For if by one man's offence death reigned by one; much more they which receive abundance of grace and of the gift of righteousness shall reign in life by one, Jesus Christ" (Rom. 5:17).

"He that spared not his own Son, but delivered him up for us all, how shall he not with him also freely give us all things?" (Rom. 8:32).

"This book of the law shall not depart out of thy mouth; but thou shalt meditate therein day and night, that thou mayest observe to do according to all that is written therein: for then thou shalt make thy way prosperous, and then thou shalt have good success" (Josh. 1:8).

"I can do all things through Christ which strengtheneth me" (Phil. 4:13).

Jehovah-nissi, "The Lord My Banner"

"And in that day there shall be a root of Jesse, which shall stand for an ensign (banner) of the people; to it shall the Gentiles seek: and his rest shall be glorious" (Is. 11:10).

"What shall we then say to these things? If God be for us, who can be against us?....Nay, in all these things we are more than conquerors through him that loved us" (Rom. 8:31,37).

"But thanks be to God, which giveth us the victory through our Lord Jesus Christ" (1 Cor. 15:57).

"But is now made manifest by the appearing of our Saviour Jesus Christ, who hath abolished death, and hath brought life and immortality to light through the gospel" (2 Tim. 1:10).

"Forasmuch then as the children are partakers of flesh and blood he also himself likewise took part of the same that through death he might destroy him that had the power of death, that is, the devil; and deliver them who through fear of death were all their lifetime subject to bondage" (Heb. 2:14,15).

"The sting of death is sin; and the strength of sin is the law. But thanks be to God, which giveth us the victory through our Lord Jesus Christ" (1 Cor. 15:56,57).

Jehovah-rohi, "The Lord My Shepherd"

"I am the good shepherd: the good shepherd giveth his life for the sheep" (John 10:11).

"Now the God of peace, that brought again from the dead our Lord Jesus, that great shepherd of the sheep, through the blood of the everlasting covenant" (Heb. 13:20).

"The Lord is my shepherd; I shall not want....Yea, though I walk through the valley of the shadow of death, I will fear no evil: for thou art with me; thy rod and thy staff they comfort me....Surely goodness and mercy shall follow me all the days of my life: and I will dwell in the house of the Lord for ever" (Ps. 23:1,4,6).

"My sheep hear my voice, and I know them, and they follow me; and I give unto them eternal life; and they shall never perish, neither shall any man pluck them out of my hand" (John 10:27,28).

II. Priorities

"Thy kingdom come. Thy will be done in earth as it is in heaven."

"Behold also the ships, which though they be so great, and are driven of fierce winds, yet are they turned about with a very small helm (rudder), whithersoever the governor listeth. Even so the tongue is a little member, and boasteth great things. Behold, how great a matter a little fire kindleth!" (James 3:4,5).

"For the kingdom of God is not meat and drink; but righteousness, and peace, and joy in the Holy Ghost" (Rom. 14:17).

"Fear not: for I am with thee: I will bring thy seed from the east, and gather thee from the west; I will say to the north, Give up; and to the south, Keep not back: bring my sons from far, and my daughters from the ends of the earth" (Is. 43:5,6).

III. Provision

"Give us this day our daily bread."

"But thou, when thou prayest, enter into thy closet, and when thou hast shut thy door pray to thy Father which is in secret; and thy Father which seeth in secret shall reward thee openly" (Matt. 6:6).

"Bring ye all the tithes into the storehouse, that there may be meat in mine house, and prove me now herewith, saith the Lord of hosts, if I will not open you the windows of heaven, and pour you out a blessing, that there shall not be room enough to receive it" (Mal. 3:10).

"Give, and it shall be given unto you; good measure, pressed down, and shaken together, and running over, shall men give into your bosom. For with the same measure that ye mete withal it shall be measured to you again" (Luke 6:38).

"But seek ye first the kingdom of God, and his righteousness; and all these things shall be added unto you" (Matt. 6:33).

"But my God shall supply all your need according to His riches in glory by Christ Jesus" (Phil. 4:19).

"Beloved, I wish above all things that thou mayest prosper and be in health, even as thy soul prospereth" (3 John 2).

IV. People

"And forgive us our debts as we forgive our debtors."

"For if ye forgive men their trespasses, your heavenly Father will also forgive you: but if ye forgive not men their trespasses, neither will your Father forgive your trespasses" (Matt. 6:14,15).

"Shouldest not thou also have had compassion on thy fellowservant, even as I had pity on thee?" (Matt. 18:33).

"But I say unto you, Love your enemies, bless them that curse you, do good to them that hate you, and pray for them which despitefully use you, and persecute you" (Matt. 5:44).

V. Power

"And lead us not into temptation, but deliver us from evil."

"Let no man say when he is tempted, I am tempted of God: for God cannot be tempted with evil, neither tempteth he any man" (James 1:13).

"My brethren, count it all joy when ye fall into divers temptations; knowing this, that the trying of your faith worketh patience. But let patience have her perfect work, that ye may be perfect and entire, wanting nothing" (James 1:2-4).

"Wherein ye greatly rejoice, though now for a season, if need be, ye are in heaviness through manifold temptations: that the trial of your faith, being much more precious than of gold that perisheth, though it be tried with fire, might be found unto praise and honour and glory at the appearing of Jesus Christ" (1 Pet. 1:6,7).

"The Lord knoweth how to deliver the godly out of temptations" (2 Pet. 2:9).

"Blessed is the man that endureth temptation: for when he is tried, he shall receive a crown of life which the Lord hath promised to them that love him" (James 1:12).

"There hath no temptation taken you but such as is common to man: but God is faithful, who will not suffer you to be tempted above that ye are able; but will with the temptation also make a way to escape, that ye may be able to bear it" (1 Cor. 10:13).

"Watch and pray, that ye enter not into temptation: the spirit indeed is willing, but the flesh is weak" (Matt. 26:41).

"Watch ye therefore, and pray always, that ye may be accounted worthy to escape all these things that shall come to pass, and to stand before the Son of man" (Luke 21:36).

VI. Praise

"For Thine is the kingdom, and the power, and the glory for ever. Amen."

"By him therefore let us offer the sacrifice of praise to God continually, that is, the fruit of our lips giving thanks to his name" (Heb. 13:15).

"In every thing give thanks: for this is the will of God in Christ Jesus concerning you" (1 Thess. 5:18).

The Kingdom

"Fear not, little flock; for it is your Father's good pleasure to give you the kingdom" (Luke 12:32).

"Giving thanks unto the Father, which hath made us meet to be partakers of the inheritance of the saints in light: who hath delivered us from the power of darkness, and hath translated us into the kingdom of his dear Son" (Col. 1:12,13).

"And the Lord shall deliver me from every evil work, and will preserve me unto his heavenly kingdom: to whom be glory for ever and ever" (2 Tim. 4:18).

The Power

"He hath made the earth by his power, he hath established the world by his wisdom, and hath stretched out the heavens by his discretion" (Jer. 10:12).

"O God, thou art terrible out of thy holy places: the God of Israel is he that giveth strength and power unto his people. Blessed be God" (Ps. 68:35).

"But thou shalt remember the Lord thy God: for it is he that giveth thee power to get wealth, that he may establish his covenant which he sware unto thy fathers, as is this day" (Deut. 8:18).

"Who are kept by the power of God through faith unto salvation ready to be revealed in the last time" (1 Pet. 1:5).

"Behold, I give unto you power to tread on serpents and scorpions, and over all the power of the enemy: and nothing shall by any means hurt you" (Luke 10:19).

"But ye shall receive power, after that the Holy Ghost is come upon you: and ye shall be witnesses unto me..." (Acts 1:8).

"Finally, my brethren, be strong in the Lord, and in the power of his might" (Eph. 6:10).

The Glory

"Glory and honour are in his presence" (1 Chron. 16:27).

"Who is this King of glory? The Lord strong and mighty, the Lord mighty in battle" (Ps. 24:8).

"But we all, with open face beholding as in a glass the glory of the Lord, are changed into the same image from glory to glory, even as by the Spirit of the Lord" (2 Cor. 3:18).

Praise be to you, O Lord,
God of our father Israel,
from everlasting to everlasting.
Yours, O Lord, is the greatness and the power
and the glory and the majesty and the splendor,
for everything in heaven and earth is yours.
Yours, O Lord, is the kingdom;
you are exalted as head over all.
Wealth and honor come from you;
you are the ruler of all things.
In your hands are strength and power
to exalt and give strength to all.
Now, our God, we give you thanks,
and praise your glorious name.

(1 Chron. 29:10-15, NIV)

How to Develop an Effective Prayer Life

To develop an effective prayer life, you must overcome these three enemies of prayer: interruptions, drowsiness and wandering thoughts. Therefore, let's learn right now how to attack and defeat them.

Interruptions

The telephone and the doorbell can become dire enemies of the believer who seeks to make a discipline of prayer. That is why many busy people choose to pray early in the morning before these distractions begin. The psalmist David had neither a telephone nor a doorbell, but he did have at least eight wives, ten concubines, twenty-two kids and a kingdom to run. It is not surprising, then, that one of David's prayer times was early in the morning! David said: "My voice shalt thou hear in the morning, O Lord; in the morning will I direct my prayer unto thee, and will look up" (Ps. 5:3).

On the other hand, Susannah Wesley, the mother of nineteen children (two of which were John and Charles Wesley who founded the Methodist movement), chose from one to two o'clock each afternoon for her time with the Lord. Every day at one o'clock, Susannah Wesley closed her bedroom door, knelt beside her bed, spread her open Bible before her and communed with God.

Think of it! There were no supermarkets, elementary schools, department stores, fast-food restaurants, laundromats or electric appliances in her day. This woman, who was also a preacher's wife, had to make the family's clothes and wash them by hand, clean up after, cook for and home school all those children, yet she made time every day for an hour with God. How would you like to try to explain to Susannah Wesley why you can't find time to pray?

Whether you choose morning, midday or evening as your prayer time, it is important that you have a set time and place to pray. Jesus, in teaching His disciples to pray, instructed: "When thou prayest, enter into thy closet, and when thou hast shut thy door, pray to thy Father which is in secret" (Matt. 6:6). This means that you need to choose a quiet, private place to pray and meet God every day. It doesn't have to be a fancy place; just a chair to kneel beside will do. But having a set time and place to pray will help defeat those interruptions.

Drowsiness

How can believers defeat the enemy of drowsiness when they pray? Some of John Wesley's early Methodist leaders who were determined to overcome this problem actually soaked towels in cold water, wrapped them around their heads and went right on praying! That's not the method I would choose, but I certainly admire their tenacity.

If you find yourself dropping off to sleep every time you kneel, cradle your head on your arm and close your eyes to pray, why not try sitting or standing? Or why not try walking as you pray? Scoot a chair or table out of the way and walk back and forth across a room or pace up and down a hall. You will grow quickly accustomed to the "path." Then you will be able to concentrate solely on prayer and defeat the enemy of drowsiness.

Wandering Thoughts

If your thoughts wander and you have difficulty concentrating as you pray, defeat that enemy by praying aloud instead of silently. Putting your thoughts into words and praying them aloud, even in a whisper, helps you focus your mind on what you're doing. Perhaps that is one of the reasons Jesus commanded: "When you pray, *say* Our Father which art in heaven..." (Luke 11:2).

Once you learn to defeat interruptions, drowsiness and wandering thoughts, within just a short time the *desire* to pray will have matured into the *discipline* to pray. And as you discipline yourself to pray, that discipline will be transformed into holy *delight*!

Don't worry if some days as you pray you shed no tears and feel no emotion. Those times you feel the least like praying may be the times you need the most to pray. Besides, God is not moved by your tears and your emotion. He is moved by His Word and your obedience and tenacity!

B.J. Willhite, our minister of prayer at Church on the Rock, who has risen to commune with God early every morning for over thirty years, explains prayer like this: "Some days you're digging holes. Some days you're planting poles. Some days you're stringing wire. And then one day the circuit is completed, and you make contact!"

God your Father promises: "When you answer the call to pray I will begin to meet all your needs." How about it? Are you ready to make a date with God each day to seek His face in prayer? Just name the time and place. He won't be late!

DATE _____

| | REQUESTS | ANSWERS |

Promises

Our Father which art in heaven, Hallowed be thy name.

Priorities

Thy kingdom come.
Thy will be done.

Provision

Give us this day our daily bread.

People

Forgive us our debts as we forgive our debtors.

Power

And lead us not into temptation, but deliver us from evil.

Praise

For thine is the kingdom, and the power, and the glory for ever. Amen.

REVELATION

DATE _____

	REQUESTS	ANSWERS

Promises

*Our Father which art in heaven,
Hallowed be thy name.*

Priorities

*Thy kingdom come.
Thy will be done.*

Provision

Give us this day our daily bread.

People

*Forgive us our debts as we
forgive our debtors.*

Power

*And lead us not into temptation,
but deliver us from evil.*

Praise

*For thine is the kingdom,
and the power, and the glory
for ever. Amen.*

REVELATION

DATE _____

REQUESTS **ANSWERS**

Promises

*Our Father which art in heaven,
Hallowed be thy name.*

Priorities

*Thy kingdom come.
Thy will be done.*

Provision

Give us this day our daily bread.

People

*Forgive us our debts as we
forgive our debtors.*

Power

*And lead us not into temptation,
but deliver us from evil.*

Praise

*For thine is the kingdom,
and the power, and the glory
for ever. Amen.*

REVELATION

DATE _____

	REQUESTS	ANSWERS

Promises

Our Father which art in heaven, Hallowed be thy name.

Priorities

Thy kingdom come.
Thy will be done.

Provision

Give us this day our daily bread.

People

Forgive us our debts as we forgive our debtors.

Power

And lead us not into temptation, but deliver us from evil.

Praise

For thine is the kingdom, and the power, and the glory for ever. Amen.

REVELATION

DATE _____

	REQUESTS	ANSWERS

Promises

Our Father which art in heaven, Hallowed be thy name.

Priorities

*Thy kingdom come.
Thy will be done.*

Provision

Give us this day our daily bread.

People

Forgive us our debts as we forgive our debtors.

Power

And lead us not into temptation, but deliver us from evil.

Praise

For thine is the kingdom, and the power, and the glory for ever. Amen.

REVELATION

DATE _____

	REQUESTS	ANSWERS

Promises

Our Father which art in heaven, Hallowed be thy name.

Priorities

Thy kingdom come.
Thy will be done.

Provision

Give us this day our daily bread.

People

Forgive us our debts as we forgive our debtors.

Power

And lead us not into temptation, but deliver us from evil.

Praise

For thine is the kingdom, and the power, and the glory for ever. Amen.

REVELATION

DATE _____

REQUESTS　　　　　**ANSWERS**

Promises
*Our Father which art in heaven,
Hallowed be thy name.*

Priorities
*Thy kingdom come.
Thy will be done.*

Provision
Give us this day our daily bread.

People
*Forgive us our debts as we
forgive our debtors.*

Power
*And lead us not into temptation,
but deliver us from evil.*

Praise
*For thine is the kingdom,
and the power, and the glory
for ever. Amen.*

REVELATION

DATE _____

	REQUESTS	ANSWERS

Promises

Our Father which art in heaven, Hallowed be thy name.

Priorities

*Thy kingdom come.
Thy will be done.*

Provision

Give us this day our daily bread.

People

Forgive us our debts as we forgive our debtors.

Power

And lead us not into temptation, but deliver us from evil.

Praise

For thine is the kingdom, and the power, and the glory for ever. Amen.

REVELATION

DATE _____

	REQUESTS	ANSWERS

Promises

Our Father which art in heaven, Hallowed be thy name.

Priorities

*Thy kingdom come.
Thy will be done.*

Provision

Give us this day our daily bread.

People

Forgive us our debts as we forgive our debtors.

Power

And lead us not into temptation, but deliver us from evil.

Praise

For thine is the kingdom, and the power, and the glory for ever. Amen.

REVELATION

DATE _____

	REQUESTS	ANSWERS

Promises
Our Father which art in heaven, Hallowed be thy name.

Priorities
Thy kingdom come.
Thy will be done.

Provision
Give us this day our daily bread.

People
Forgive us our debts as we forgive our debtors.

Power
And lead us not into temptation, but deliver us from evil.

Praise
For thine is the kingdom, and the power, and the glory for ever. Amen.

REVELATION

DATE _____

	REQUESTS	ANSWERS

Promises
Our Father which art in heaven,
Hallowed be thy name.

Priorities
Thy kingdom come.
Thy will be done.

Provision
Give us this day our daily bread.

People
Forgive us our debts as we
forgive our debtors.

Power
And lead us not into temptation,
but deliver us from evil.

Praise
For thine is the kingdom,
and the power, and the glory
for ever. Amen.

REVELATION

DATE _____

	REQUESTS	ANSWERS

Promises
Our Father which art in heaven, Hallowed be thy name.

Priorities
*Thy kingdom come.
Thy will be done.*

Provision
Give us this day our daily bread.

People
Forgive us our debts as we forgive our debtors.

Power
And lead us not into temptation, but deliver us from evil.

Praise
For thine is the kingdom, and the power, and the glory for ever. Amen.

REVELATION

DATE _____

REQUESTS	ANSWERS

Promises
Our Father which art in heaven, Hallowed be thy name.

Priorities
Thy kingdom come.
Thy will be done.

Provision
Give us this day our daily bread.

People
Forgive us our debts as we forgive our debtors.

Power
And lead us not into temptation, but deliver us from evil.

Praise
For thine is the kingdom, and the power, and the glory for ever. Amen.

REVELATION

DATE _____

	REQUESTS	ANSWERS

Promises
Our Father which art in heaven,
Hallowed be thy name.

Priorities
Thy kingdom come.
Thy will be done.

Provision
Give us this day our daily bread.

People
Forgive us our debts as we
forgive our debtors.

Power
And lead us not into temptation,
but deliver us from evil.

Praise
For thine is the kingdom,
and the power, and the glory
for ever. Amen.

REVELATION

DATE _____

	REQUESTS	ANSWERS

Promises
Our Father which art in heaven, Hallowed be thy name.

Priorities
*Thy kingdom come.
Thy will be done.*

Provision
Give us this day our daily bread.

People
Forgive us our debts as we forgive our debtors.

Power
And lead us not into temptation, but deliver us from evil.

Praise
For thine is the kingdom, and the power, and the glory for ever. Amen.

REVELATION

DATE _____

	REQUESTS	ANSWERS

Promises
Our Father which art in heaven, Hallowed be thy name.

Priorities
*Thy kingdom come.
Thy will be done.*

Provision
Give us this day our daily bread.

People
Forgive us our debts as we forgive our debtors.

Power
And lead us not into temptation, but deliver us from evil.

Praise
For thine is the kingdom, and the power, and the glory for ever. Amen.

REVELATION

DATE _____

	REQUESTS	ANSWERS

Promises
Our Father which art in heaven,
Hallowed be thy name.

Priorities
Thy kingdom come.
Thy will be done.

Provision
Give us this day our daily bread.

People
Forgive us our debts as we
forgive our debtors.

Power
And lead us not into temptation,
but deliver us from evil.

Praise
For thine is the kingdom,
and the power, and the glory
for ever. Amen.

REVELATION

DATE _____

REQUESTS **ANSWERS**

Promises
Our Father which art in heaven, Hallowed be thy name.

Priorities
Thy kingdom come.
Thy will be done.

Provision
Give us this day our daily bread.

People
Forgive us our debts as we forgive our debtors.

Power
And lead us not into temptation, but deliver us from evil.

Praise
For thine is the kingdom, and the power, and the glory for ever. Amen.

REVELATION

DATE _____

	REQUESTS	ANSWERS

Promises
*Our Father which art in heaven,
Hallowed be thy name.*

Priorities
*Thy kingdom come.
Thy will be done.*

Provision
Give us this day our daily bread.

People
*Forgive us our debts as we
forgive our debtors.*

Power
*And lead us not into temptation,
but deliver us from evil.*

Praise
*For thine is the kingdom,
and the power, and the glory
for ever. Amen.*

REVELATION

DATE _____

REQUESTS　　　　　ANSWERS

Promises

*Our Father which art in heaven,
Hallowed be thy name.*

Priorities

*Thy kingdom come.
Thy will be done.*

Provision

Give us this day our daily bread.

People

*Forgive us our debts as we
forgive our debtors.*

Power

*And lead us not into temptation,
but deliver us from evil.*

Praise

*For thine is the kingdom,
and the power, and the glory
for ever. Amen.*

REVELATION

DATE _____

	REQUESTS	ANSWERS

Promises

*Our Father which art in heaven,
Hallowed be thy name.*

Priorities

*Thy kingdom come.
Thy will be done.*

Provision

Give us this day our daily bread.

People

*Forgive us our debts as we
forgive our debtors.*

Power

*And lead us not into temptation,
but deliver us from evil.*

Praise

*For thine is the kingdom,
and the power, and the glory
for ever. Amen.*

REVELATION

DATE _____

	REQUESTS	ANSWERS

Promises
Our Father which art in heaven,
Hallowed be thy name.

Priorities
Thy kingdom come.
Thy will be done.

Provision
Give us this day our daily bread.

People
Forgive us our debts as we
forgive our debtors.

Power
And lead us not into temptation,
but deliver us from evil.

Praise
For thine is the kingdom,
and the power, and the glory
for ever. Amen.

REVELATION

DATE _____

REQUESTS **ANSWERS**

Promises

*Our Father which art in heaven,
Hallowed be thy name.*

Priorities

*Thy kingdom come.
Thy will be done.*

Provision

Give us this day our daily bread.

People

*Forgive us our debts as we
forgive our debtors.*

Power

*And lead us not into temptation,
but deliver us from evil.*

Praise

*For thine is the kingdom,
and the power, and the glory
for ever. Amen.*

REVELATION

DATE _____

	REQUESTS	ANSWERS

Promises
Our Father which art in heaven, Hallowed be thy name.

Priorities
*Thy kingdom come.
Thy will be done.*

Provision
Give us this day our daily bread.

People
Forgive us our debts as we forgive our debtors.

Power
And lead us not into temptation, but deliver us from evil.

Praise
For thine is the kingdom, and the power, and the glory for ever. Amen.

REVELATION

DATE _____

	REQUESTS	ANSWERS

Promises
Our Father which art in heaven, Hallowed be thy name.

Priorities
*Thy kingdom come.
Thy will be done.*

Provision
Give us this day our daily bread.

People
Forgive us our debts as we forgive our debtors.

Power
And lead us not into temptation, but deliver us from evil.

Praise
For thine is the kingdom, and the power, and the glory for ever. Amen.

REVELATION

DATE _____

REQUESTS **ANSWERS**

Promises

*Our Father which art in heaven,
Hallowed be thy name.*

Priorities

*Thy kingdom come.
Thy will be done.*

Provision

Give us this day our daily bread.

People

*Forgive us our debts as we
forgive our debtors.*

Power

*And lead us not into temptation,
but deliver us from evil.*

Praise

*For thine is the kingdom,
and the power, and the glory
for ever. Amen.*

REVELATION

DATE _____

	REQUESTS	ANSWERS

Promises
Our Father which art in heaven, Hallowed be thy name.

Priorities
*Thy kingdom come.
Thy will be done.*

Provision
Give us this day our daily bread.

People
Forgive us our debts as we forgive our debtors.

Power
And lead us not into temptation, but deliver us from evil.

Praise
For thine is the kingdom, and the power, and the glory for ever. Amen.

REVELATION

DATE _____

REQUESTS   **ANSWERS**

Promises
*Our Father which art in heaven,
Hallowed be thy name.*

Priorities
*Thy kingdom come.
Thy will be done.*

Provision
Give us this day our daily bread.

People
*Forgive us our debts as we
forgive our debtors.*

Power
*And lead us not into temptation,
but deliver us from evil.*

Praise
*For thine is the kingdom,
and the power, and the glory
for ever. Amen.*

REVELATION

DATE _____

                                  REQUESTS   **ANSWERS**

Promises

Our Father which art in heaven,
Hallowed be thy name.

Priorities

Thy kingdom come.
Thy will be done.

Provision

Give us this day our daily bread.

People

Forgive us our debts as we
forgive our debtors.

Power

And lead us not into temptation,
but deliver us from evil.

Praise

For thine is the kingdom,
and the power, and the glory
for ever. Amen.

REVELATION

DATE _____

| REQUESTS | ANSWERS |

Promises
*Our Father which art in heaven,
Hallowed be thy name.*

Priorities
*Thy kingdom come.
Thy will be done.*

Provision
Give us this day our daily bread.

People
*Forgive us our debts as we
forgive our debtors.*

Power
*And lead us not into temptation,
but deliver us from evil.*

Praise
*For thine is the kingdom,
and the power, and the glory
for ever. Amen.*

REVELATION

DATE _____

	REQUESTS	ANSWERS

Promises

Our Father which art in heaven, Hallowed be thy name.

Priorities

Thy kingdom come.
Thy will be done.

Provision

Give us this day our daily bread.

People

Forgive us our debts as we forgive our debtors.

Power

And lead us not into temptation, but deliver us from evil.

Praise

For thine is the kingdom, and the power, and the glory for ever. Amen.

REVELATION

DATE _____

	REQUESTS	ANSWERS

Promises
Our Father which art in heaven, Hallowed be thy name.

Priorities
Thy kingdom come.
Thy will be done.

Provision
Give us this day our daily bread.

People
Forgive us our debts as we forgive our debtors.

Power
And lead us not into temptation, but deliver us from evil.

Praise
For thine is the kingdom, and the power, and the glory for ever. Amen.

REVELATION

DATE _____

	REQUESTS	ANSWERS

Promises

Our Father which art in heaven, Hallowed be thy name.

Priorities

*Thy kingdom come.
Thy will be done.*

Provision

Give us this day our daily bread.

People

Forgive us our debts as we forgive our debtors.

Power

And lead us not into temptation, but deliver us from evil.

Praise

For thine is the kingdom, and the power, and the glory for ever. Amen.

REVELATION

DATE _____

	REQUESTS	ANSWERS

Promises

Our Father which art in heaven, Hallowed be thy name.

Priorities

*Thy kingdom come.
Thy will be done.*

Provision

Give us this day our daily bread.

People

Forgive us our debts as we forgive our debtors.

Power

And lead us not into temptation, but deliver us from evil.

Praise

For thine is the kingdom, and the power, and the glory for ever. Amen.

REVELATION

DATE _____

                                REQUESTS   **ANSWERS**

Promises
*Our Father which art in heaven,
Hallowed be thy name.*

Priorities
*Thy kingdom come.
Thy will be done.*

Provision
Give us this day our daily bread.

People
*Forgive us our debts as we
forgive our debtors.*

Power
*And lead us not into temptation,
but deliver us from evil.*

Praise
*For thine is the kingdom,
and the power, and the glory
for ever. Amen.*

REVELATION

DATE _____

REQUESTS | ANSWERS

Promises
Our Father which art in heaven, Hallowed be thy name.

Priorities
Thy kingdom come.
Thy will be done.

Provision
Give us this day our daily bread.

People
Forgive us our debts as we forgive our debtors.

Power
And lead us not into temptation, but deliver us from evil.

Praise
For thine is the kingdom, and the power, and the glory for ever. Amen.

REVELATION

DATE _____

	REQUESTS	ANSWERS

Promises
Our Father which art in heaven, Hallowed be thy name.

Priorities
Thy kingdom come.
Thy will be done.

Provision
Give us this day our daily bread.

People
Forgive us our debts as we forgive our debtors.

Power
And lead us not into temptation, but deliver us from evil.

Praise
For thine is the kingdom, and the power, and the glory for ever. Amen.

REVELATION

DATE _____

REQUESTS **ANSWERS**

Promises

Our Father which art in heaven, Hallowed be thy name.

Priorities

*Thy kingdom come.
Thy will be done.*

Provision

Give us this day our daily bread.

People

Forgive us our debts as we forgive our debtors.

Power

And lead us not into temptation, but deliver us from evil.

Praise

For thine is the kingdom, and the power, and the glory for ever. Amen.

REVELATION

DATE _____

REQUESTS **ANSWERS**

Promises
Our Father which art in heaven, Hallowed be thy name.

Priorities
*Thy kingdom come.
Thy will be done.*

Provision
Give us this day our daily bread.

People
Forgive us our debts as we forgive our debtors.

Power
And lead us not into temptation, but deliver us from evil.

Praise
For thine is the kingdom, and the power, and the glory for ever. Amen.

REVELATION

DATE _____

	REQUESTS	ANSWERS

Promises
Our Father which art in heaven,
Hallowed be thy name.

Priorities
Thy kingdom come.
Thy will be done.

Provision
Give us this day our daily bread.

People
Forgive us our debts as we
forgive our debtors.

Power
And lead us not into temptation,
but deliver us from evil.

Praise
For thine is the kingdom,
and the power, and the glory
for ever. Amen.

REVELATION

DATE _____

	REQUESTS	ANSWERS

Promises
Our Father which art in heaven,
Hallowed be thy name.

Priorities
Thy kingdom come.
Thy will be done.

Provision
Give us this day our daily bread.

People
Forgive us our debts as we
forgive our debtors.

Power
And lead us not into temptation,
but deliver us from evil.

Praise
For thine is the kingdom,
and the power, and the glory
for ever. Amen.

REVELATION

DATE _____

	REQUESTS	ANSWERS

Promises
Our Father which art in heaven, Hallowed be thy name.

Priorities
*Thy kingdom come.
Thy will be done.*

Provision
Give us this day our daily bread.

People
Forgive us our debts as we forgive our debtors.

Power
And lead us not into temptation, but deliver us from evil.

Praise
For thine is the kingdom, and the power, and the glory for ever. Amen.

REVELATION

DATE _____

REQUESTS   ANSWERS

Promises
Our Father which art in heaven, Hallowed be thy name.

Priorities
*Thy kingdom come.
Thy will be done.*

Provision
Give us this day our daily bread.

People
Forgive us our debts as we forgive our debtors.

Power
And lead us not into temptation, but deliver us from evil.

Praise
For thine is the kingdom, and the power, and the glory for ever. Amen.

REVELATION

DATE _____

　　　　　　　　　　　REQUESTS　　　　　　ANSWERS

Promises

*Our Father which art in heaven,
Hallowed be thy name.*

Priorities

*Thy kingdom come.
Thy will be done.*

Provision

Give us this day our daily bread.

People

*Forgive us our debts as we
forgive our debtors.*

Power

*And lead us not into temptation,
but deliver us from evil.*

Praise

*For thine is the kingdom,
and the power, and the glory
for ever. Amen.*

REVELATION

DATE _____

	REQUESTS	ANSWERS

Promises
Our Father which art in heaven,
Hallowed be thy name.

Priorities
Thy kingdom come.
Thy will be done.

Provision
Give us this day our daily bread.

People
Forgive us our debts as we
forgive our debtors.

Power
And lead us not into temptation,
but deliver us from evil.

Praise
For thine is the kingdom,
and the power, and the glory
for ever. Amen.

REVELATION

DATE _____

	REQUESTS	ANSWERS

Promises
Our Father which art in heaven,
Hallowed be thy name.

Priorities
Thy kingdom come.
Thy will be done.

Provision
Give us this day our daily bread.

People
Forgive us our debts as we
forgive our debtors.

Power
And lead us not into temptation,
but deliver us from evil.

Praise
For thine is the kingdom,
and the power, and the glory
for ever. Amen.

REVELATION

DATE _____

REQUESTS　　　　　**ANSWERS**

Promises

Our Father which art in heaven, Hallowed be thy name.

Priorities

*Thy kingdom come.
Thy will be done.*

Provision

Give us this day our daily bread.

People

Forgive us our debts as we forgive our debtors.

Power

And lead us not into temptation, but deliver us from evil.

Praise

For thine is the kingdom, and the power, and the glory for ever. Amen.

REVELATION

DATE _____

	REQUESTS	ANSWERS

Promises

*Our Father which art in heaven,
Hallowed be thy name.*

Priorities

*Thy kingdom come.
Thy will be done.*

Provision

Give us this day our daily bread.

People

*Forgive us our debts as we
forgive our debtors.*

Power

*And lead us not into temptation,
but deliver us from evil.*

Praise

*For thine is the kingdom,
and the power, and the glory
for ever. Amen.*

REVELATION

DATE _____

REQUESTS **ANSWERS**

Promises

*Our Father which art in heaven,
Hallowed be thy name.*

Priorities

*Thy kingdom come.
Thy will be done.*

Provision

Give us this day our daily bread.

People

*Forgive us our debts as we
forgive our debtors.*

Power

*And lead us not into temptation,
but deliver us from evil.*

Praise

*For thine is the kingdom,
and the power, and the glory
for ever. Amen.*

REVELATION

DATE _____

	REQUESTS	ANSWERS

Promises

Our Father which art in heaven, Hallowed be thy name.

Priorities

*Thy kingdom come.
Thy will be done.*

Provision

Give us this day our daily bread.

People

Forgive us our debts as we forgive our debtors.

Power

And lead us not into temptation, but deliver us from evil.

Praise

For thine is the kingdom, and the power, and the glory for ever. Amen.

REVELATION

DATE _____

	REQUESTS	ANSWERS

Promises
Our Father which art in heaven, Hallowed be thy name.

Priorities
*Thy kingdom come.
Thy will be done.*

Provision
Give us this day our daily bread.

People
Forgive us our debts as we forgive our debtors.

Power
And lead us not into temptation, but deliver us from evil.

Praise
For thine is the kingdom, and the power, and the glory for ever. Amen.

REVELATION

DATE _____

	REQUESTS	ANSWERS

Promises

*Our Father which art in heaven,
Hallowed be thy name.*

Priorities

*Thy kingdom come.
Thy will be done.*

Provision

Give us this day our daily bread.

People

*Forgive us our debts as we
forgive our debtors.*

Power

*And lead us not into temptation,
but deliver us from evil.*

Praise

*For thine is the kingdom,
and the power, and the glory
for ever. Amen.*

REVELATION

DATE _____

	REQUESTS	ANSWERS

Promises

*Our Father which art in heaven,
Hallowed be thy name.*

Priorities

*Thy kingdom come.
Thy will be done.*

Provision

Give us this day our daily bread.

People

*Forgive us our debts as we
forgive our debtors.*

Power

*And lead us not into temptation,
but deliver us from evil.*

Praise

*For thine is the kingdom,
and the power, and the glory
for ever. Amen.*

REVELATION

DATE _____

	REQUESTS	ANSWERS

Promises

*Our Father which art in heaven,
Hallowed be thy name.*

Priorities

*Thy kingdom come.
Thy will be done.*

Provision

Give us this day our daily bread.

People

*Forgive us our debts as we
forgive our debtors.*

Power

*And lead us not into temptation,
but deliver us from evil.*

Praise

*For thine is the kingdom,
and the power, and the glory
for ever. Amen.*

REVELATION

DATE _____

	REQUESTS	ANSWERS

Promises
Our Father which art in heaven, Hallowed be thy name.

Priorities
*Thy kingdom come.
Thy will be done.*

Provision
Give us this day our daily bread.

People
Forgive us our debts as we forgive our debtors.

Power
And lead us not into temptation, but deliver us from evil.

Praise
For thine is the kingdom, and the power, and the glory for ever. Amen.

REVELATION

DATE _____

	REQUESTS	ANSWERS

Promises
Our Father which art in heaven, Hallowed be thy name.

Priorities
*Thy kingdom come.
Thy will be done.*

Provision
Give us this day our daily bread.

People
Forgive us our debts as we forgive our debtors.

Power
And lead us not into temptation, but deliver us from evil.

Praise
For thine is the kingdom, and the power, and the glory for ever. Amen.

REVELATION

DATE _____

REQUESTS	ANSWERS

Promises
Our Father which art in heaven, Hallowed be thy name.

Priorities
Thy kingdom come.
Thy will be done.

Provision
Give us this day our daily bread.

People
Forgive us our debts as we forgive our debtors.

Power
And lead us not into temptation, but deliver us from evil.

Praise
For thine is the kingdom, and the power, and the glory for ever. Amen.

REVELATION

DATE _____

REQUESTS	ANSWERS

Promises

Our Father which art in heaven, Hallowed be thy name.

Priorities

Thy kingdom come.
Thy will be done.

Provision

Give us this day our daily bread.

People

Forgive us our debts as we forgive our debtors.

Power

And lead us not into temptation, but deliver us from evil.

Praise

For thine is the kingdom, and the power, and the glory for ever. Amen.

REVELATION

DATE _____

	REQUESTS	ANSWERS

Promises

Our Father which art in heaven, Hallowed be thy name.

Priorities

*Thy kingdom come.
Thy will be done.*

Provision

Give us this day our daily bread.

People

Forgive us our debts as we forgive our debtors.

Power

And lead us not into temptation, but deliver us from evil.

Praise

For thine is the kingdom, and the power, and the glory for ever. Amen.

REVELATION

DATE _____

	REQUESTS	ANSWERS

Promises

*Our Father which art in heaven,
Hallowed be thy name.*

Priorities

*Thy kingdom come.
Thy will be done.*

Provision

Give us this day our daily bread.

People

*Forgive us our debts as we
forgive our debtors.*

Power

*And lead us not into temptation,
but deliver us from evil.*

Praise

*For thine is the kingdom,
and the power, and the glory
for ever. Amen.*

REVELATION

DATE _____

	REQUESTS	ANSWERS

Promises

Our Father which art in heaven, Hallowed be thy name.

Priorities

Thy kingdom come.
Thy will be done.

Provision

Give us this day our daily bread.

People

Forgive us our debts as we forgive our debtors.

Power

And lead us not into temptation, but deliver us from evil.

Praise

For thine is the kingdom, and the power, and the glory for ever. Amen.

REVELATION

DATE _____

	REQUESTS	ANSWERS

Promises
*Our Father which art in heaven,
Hallowed be thy name.*

Priorities
*Thy kingdom come.
Thy will be done.*

Provision
Give us this day our daily bread.

People
*Forgive us our debts as we
forgive our debtors.*

Power
*And lead us not into temptation,
but deliver us from evil.*

Praise
*For thine is the kingdom,
and the power, and the glory
for ever. Amen.*

REVELATION

DATE _____

                         REQUESTS   **ANSWERS**

Promises

*Our Father which art in heaven,
Hallowed be thy name.*

Priorities

*Thy kingdom come.
Thy will be done.*

Provision

Give us this day our daily bread.

People

*Forgive us our debts as we
forgive our debtors.*

Power

*And lead us not into temptation,
but deliver us from evil.*

Praise

*For thine is the kingdom,
and the power, and the glory
for ever. Amen.*

REVELATION

DATE _____

	REQUESTS	ANSWERS

Promises

Our Father which art in heaven, Hallowed be thy name.

Priorities

Thy kingdom come.
Thy will be done.

Provision

Give us this day our daily bread.

People

Forgive us our debts as we forgive our debtors.

Power

And lead us not into temptation, but deliver us from evil.

Praise

For thine is the kingdom, and the power, and the glory for ever. Amen.

REVELATION

DATE _____

REQUESTS **ANSWERS**

Promises

*Our Father which art in heaven,
Hallowed be thy name.*

Priorities

*Thy kingdom come.
Thy will be done.*

Provision

Give us this day our daily bread.

People

*Forgive us our debts as we
forgive our debtors.*

Power

*And lead us not into temptation,
but deliver us from evil.*

Praise

*For thine is the kingdom,
and the power, and the glory
for ever. Amen.*

REVELATION

DATE _____

| | REQUESTS | ANSWERS |

Promises

*Our Father which art in heaven,
Hallowed be thy name.*

Priorities

*Thy kingdom come.
Thy will be done.*

Provision

Give us this day our daily bread.

People

*Forgive us our debts as we
forgive our debtors.*

Power

*And lead us not into temptation,
but deliver us from evil.*

Praise

*For thine is the kingdom,
and the power, and the glory
for ever. Amen.*

REVELATION

DATE _____

	REQUESTS	ANSWERS

Promises

*Our Father which art in heaven,
Hallowed be thy name.*

Priorities

*Thy kingdom come.
Thy will be done.*

Provision

Give us this day our daily bread.

People

*Forgive us our debts as we
forgive our debtors.*

Power

*And lead us not into temptation,
but deliver us from evil.*

Praise

*For thine is the kingdom,
and the power, and the glory
for ever. Amen.*

REVELATION

DATE _____

REQUESTS   **ANSWERS**

Promises
Our Father which art in heaven,
Hallowed be thy name.

Priorities
Thy kingdom come.
Thy will be done.

Provision
Give us this day our daily bread.

People
Forgive us our debts as we
forgive our debtors.

Power
And lead us not into temptation,
but deliver us from evil.

Praise
For thine is the kingdom,
and the power, and the glory
for ever. Amen.

REVELATION

DATE _____

	REQUESTS	ANSWERS

Promises

*Our Father which art in heaven,
Hallowed be thy name.*

Priorities

*Thy kingdom come.
Thy will be done.*

Provision

Give us this day our daily bread.

People

*Forgive us our debts as we
forgive our debtors.*

Power

*And lead us not into temptation,
but deliver us from evil.*

Praise

*For thine is the kingdom,
and the power, and the glory
for ever. Amen.*

REVELATION

DATE _____

	REQUESTS	ANSWERS

Promises

Our Father which art in heaven, Hallowed be thy name.

Priorities

Thy kingdom come.
Thy will be done.

Provision

Give us this day our daily bread.

People

Forgive us our debts as we forgive our debtors.

Power

And lead us not into temptation, but deliver us from evil.

Praise

For thine is the kingdom, and the power, and the glory for ever. Amen.

REVELATION

DATE _____

	REQUESTS	ANSWERS

Promises

*Our Father which art in heaven,
Hallowed be thy name.*

Priorities

*Thy kingdom come.
Thy will be done.*

Provision

Give us this day our daily bread.

People

*Forgive us our debts as we
forgive our debtors.*

Power

*And lead us not into temptation,
but deliver us from evil.*

Praise

*For thine is the kingdom,
and the power, and the glory
for ever. Amen.*

REVELATION

DATE _____

REQUESTS   **ANSWERS**

Promises

*Our Father which art in heaven,
Hallowed be thy name.*

Priorities

*Thy kingdom come.
Thy will be done.*

Provision

Give us this day our daily bread.

People

*Forgive us our debts as we
forgive our debtors.*

Power

*And lead us not into temptation,
but deliver us from evil.*

Praise

*For thine is the kingdom,
and the power, and the glory
for ever. Amen.*

REVELATION

DATE _____

	REQUESTS	ANSWERS

Promises

Our Father which art in heaven, Hallowed be thy name.

Priorities

*Thy kingdom come.
Thy will be done.*

Provision

Give us this day our daily bread.

People

Forgive us our debts as we forgive our debtors.

Power

And lead us not into temptation, but deliver us from evil.

Praise

For thine is the kingdom, and the power, and the glory for ever. Amen.

REVELATION

DATE _____

	REQUESTS	ANSWERS

Promises

Our Father which art in heaven, Hallowed be thy name.

Priorities

Thy kingdom come.
Thy will be done.

Provision

Give us this day our daily bread.

People

Forgive us our debts as we forgive our debtors.

Power

And lead us not into temptation, but deliver us from evil.

Praise

For thine is the kingdom, and the power, and the glory for ever. Amen.

REVELATION

DATE _____

	REQUESTS	ANSWERS

Promises
Our Father which art in heaven, Hallowed be thy name.

Priorities
Thy kingdom come.
Thy will be done.

Provision
Give us this day our daily bread.

People
Forgive us our debts as we forgive our debtors.

Power
And lead us not into temptation, but deliver us from evil.

Praise
For thine is the kingdom, and the power, and the glory for ever. Amen.

REVELATION

DATE _____

	REQUESTS	ANSWERS

Promises

*Our Father which art in heaven,
Hallowed be thy name.*

Priorities

*Thy kingdom come.
Thy will be done.*

Provision

Give us this day our daily bread.

People

*Forgive us our debts as we
forgive our debtors.*

Power

*And lead us not into temptation,
but deliver us from evil.*

Praise

*For thine is the kingdom,
and the power, and the glory
for ever. Amen.*

REVELATION

How to Read the Bible Through in One Year

John Bunyan, the author of *Pilgrim's Progress*, said of the Bible: "This Book will keep you from sin, or sin will keep you from this Book." Bunyan was right! Therefore, it is essential that believers read the Word of God daily and learn to require it as a vital necessity.

Did you know that you can read the entire Bible through in one year by reading fifteen minutes each day or three chapters every weekday and five on Sunday? If you choose that simple, effective method of reading the Bible through, use this chart to check each chapter and record your progress as you read the Bible daily.

Remember this: The Bible is the Word of God. Treasure it. Study it. Obey it. As you do, God's Word will be a source of light, hope and strength all the days of your life!

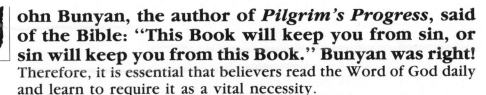

How to Pray for Missionaries and Other Christian Leaders

The apostle Paul, a man of prayer, prayed for his many converts and for the new churches established under his ministry, but Paul also taught those believers to pray for him. He urged, "Brethren, pray for us" (1 Thess. 5:25). He wrote to the Corinthian believers who were, in Paul's words, "helping together by prayer for us" (2 Cor. 1:11). You see, a praying person is a partner with the missionary, "helping together." Paul literally begged believers to pray for him: "Now I beseech you, brethren, for the Lord Jesus Christ's sake, and for the love of the Spirit, that ye strive together with me in your prayers to God for me" (Rom. 15:30).

In his letters, Paul not only requested that believers pray for him in prison and on his missionary journeys; he also gave specific requests for which they were to pray. Therefore, believers today can learn how to pray effectively for missionaries and other Christian leaders by remembering seven specific prayer requests recorded by Paul in his epistles.

1. Pray for Open Doors.

"Continue earnestly in prayer, being vigilant in it with thanksgiving; meanwhile praying also for us, that God would open to us a door for the word, to speak the mystery of Christ..." (Col. 4:2,3, NIV).

Open doors cannot be taken for granted; therefore, missionaries and Christian leaders must be sensitive to the Lord's leading. Pray that Christian workers will be led by the Holy Spirit to prepared hearts which will receive the Word and the servants of God who bring that Word. Pray that God will open doors of opportunity, doors of ministry, doors of blessing and doors of friendship, and that the servants of God will recognize and step through those open doors.

2. Pray for Boldness.

"Praying always with all prayer and supplication in the Spirit, being watchful to this end with all perseverance and supplication for all the saints—and for me, that utterance may be given to me, that I may open my mouth boldly to make known the mystery of the gospel" (Eph. 6:18,19, NIV).

Paul asks three different times in his epistles that believers pray that he will have boldness. Why was boldness so important to Paul? Why should we pray that missionaries and Christian leaders will have boldness?

- Attempting to function effectively in a strange culture, in a strange language and in settings to which one is unaccustomed requires boldness.
- Overcoming the opposition of evil forces requires boldness.
- Overcoming the fear of failure and fear of embarrassment requires boldness.
- Moving forward by faith into unknown, undeveloped areas requires boldness.

3. Pray That the Word of God Will Have Free Course.

"Finally, brethren, pray for us, that the word of the Lord may have free course and be glorified" (2 Thess. 3:1, NIV).

Obstacles have to be removed if the Word of God is to flow freely. If the Word of God is to go forward unobstructed, Satan, who is determined to obstruct the free flow of the gospel, must be bound (James 4:7; Eph. 6:10-18). The weary arms of Christian workers must be uplifted by intercessors, and closed minds and hearts must be opened to pay attention to the Word of God. We must address these areas in prayer if the Word of God is to have free course.

4. Pray for Protection and Deliverance.

"Pray...that we may be delivered from unreasonable and wicked men; for not all have faith" (2 Thess. 3:2, NIV).

How was Paul delivered from stonings, shipwrecks, beatings, whippings, mobs and snakebite? Believers were praying for his safety!

Christian workers need prayer for protection and deliverance from Satan's murderous onslaughts and from wicked people who are capable of outrageous, unreasonable conduct.

5. Pray the Worker's Ministry Will Be Accepted by Believers.

"Pray...that my service (ministry) for Jerusalem may be acceptable to the saints" (Rom. 15:31, NIV).

If believers do not heartily welcome and accept a Christian worker's ministry, his work will be hindered. Cooperation, as well as emotional and financial support, may be withheld. Therefore, believers should pray that the worker's ministry will be worthy to be received, and that the believers for whom that worker labors will appreciate and receive his or her ministry.

6. Pray for Divine Guidance and Assistance in Travel.

"Pray...that I may come to you with joy by the will of God" (Rom. 15:32, NIV).

Most missionaries and Christian leaders are constantly traveling, and their mode of transportation varies: jets, ships, helicopters, boats, canoes, buses, horses, bicycles, jeeps—even hiking.

Often these travels involve stressful situations: great distances, border crossings, obtaining visas and money for tickets, bad weather, robberies or life-threatening situations engineered by political activists.

Therefore, believers must not forget to pray for the **protection, provision, timing and permission** urgently needed by Christian workers as they travel.

7. Pray for Refreshment.

"Pray that I...may be refreshed together with you" (Rom. 15:32b, NIV).

Loneliness, fatigue, health problems, discouragement and disappointments may cause the missionary or Christian leader to doubt God or the call of God upon his or her life. Therefore, believers should pray that Christian workers will seek and receive refreshing infillings of the Holy Spirit and that the workers will develop discipline in studying God's Word and in maintaining effective, consistent prayer lives.

In addition, believers should pray that Christian workers will be enabled to exchange rich, spiritual fellowship with other believers, and that the necessary time and finances for spiritual retreats and urgently needed vacations will be made available.

And don't forget: A letter, gift, tape or book from a "praying helper" might be used by the Spirit to bring refreshment to a Christian worker's weary spirit.

Paul was himself a missionary and Christian leader, so he knew a Christian worker's greatest needs. Let's take Paul's seven personal prayer requests and turn them into specific, effective petitions for other missionaries and Christian leaders who also are begging, "Brethren, pray for us!"

By Wayne Huff, regional director for Wycliffe Bible Translators and former missionary to Guatemala.

Africa

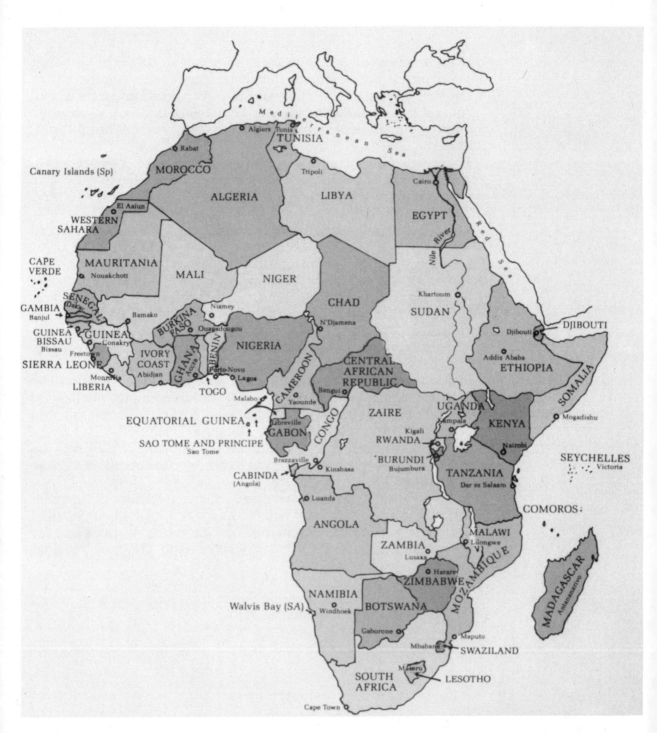

Asia

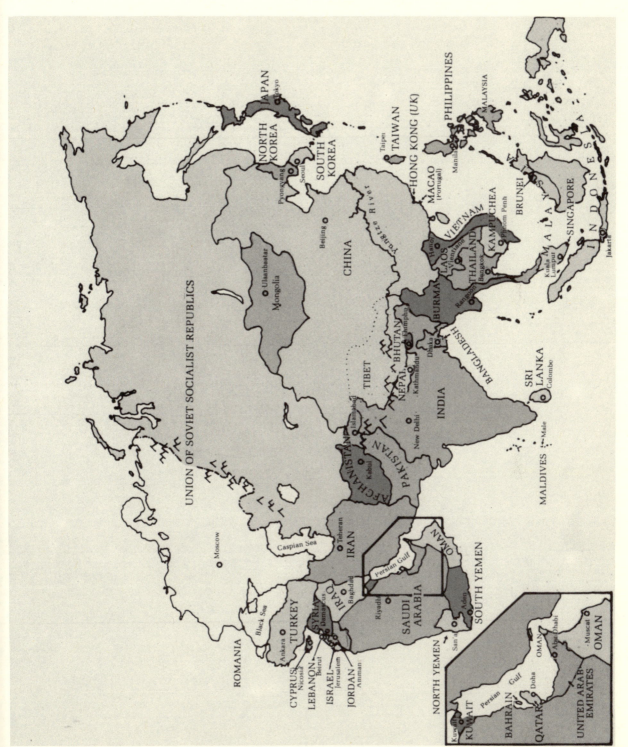

Europe

South America

North America

Biography

Larry Lea is pastor of the Church on the Rock, Rockwall, Texas. By 1987, the church had added 11,000 members to the 13 people who first gathered in 1980. Lea attributes this phenomenal growth to the members' praying an hour daily, interceding for new Christians.

Lea is also dean of the seminary at Oral Roberts University, Tulsa, Oklahoma. His weekly television program, "Change Your Life," appears on the PTL network. He writes Let's Pray, a monthly column in *Charisma* magazine.